A HEINEMANN EASY-TO-READ BOOK

Maureen Osborne

The Horrobilly Goes to School

Pictures by Eileen Browne

Heinemann : London

By the same author and artist
Here Comes the Horrobilly

For Maurice

Reading consultant: Mary M Hoffman
First published 1979

434 95582 5

William Heinemann Ltd
15 Queen Street, Mayfair, London W1X 8BE
LONDON MELBOURNE TORONTO
JOHANNESBURG AUCKLAND

Printed in Great Britain by
Caledonian Graphics Ltd

The Horrobilly lived
with his friend Captain Sam
in Hairy Mary's cottage.
She was their landlady.
She was called Hairy Mary
because her hair
stuck out like a mop.

The Horrobilly tried
to be friends with Hairy Mary.
It wasn't easy.
About most things
they did not agree.
She did not like his pet mice.

He did not like her bad temper.
She said he was lazy.
He said she was bossy.
One morning she said,
"Get dressed, Horrobilly.
You must go to school today."

"Sh! Not so loud,"
said the Horrobilly.
"Can't you see I'm asleep?
Please leave the room."
"Rubbish!" said Hairy Mary crossly.
"Get up at once.
I'm in a hurry.
I'm starting a new job today."

The Horrobilly made
a few sandwiches
for his dinner.

But he ate most of them
on the way to school.
He was so busy eating
he didn't notice
his pet mice following him.

At school, the children
told the Horrobilly
where to put his dinner.
"Hurry up," they said.
"There's a new teacher today."

It was Hairy Mary.

"I'm the new teacher," she said.

"This is my new job.

And for my first lesson

I will teach you how to spell."

Then Hairy Mary saw
the Horrobilly's mice.
So she wrote "No mice"
on the blackboard.
"Copy the letters
and learn to spell,"
she said.

The Horrobilly wrote
the right letters,
but he got them
in the wrong order.
The children laughed,
but Hairy Mary was furious.

"Hairy Mary said it was a spell,"
the Horrobilly said to himself.
"I'll shut my eyes
and try to change her
into something."

While his eyes were shut
Hairy Mary went out.
When he opened them
he saw that the spell had worked.
"I **am** clever," he said.

But the Horrobilly wasn't sure
he liked magic after all.
He climbed on to the cupboard
to be safe.
"I wouldn't like a cat
to get you, Hairy Mary.

But it serves you right
for being so grumpy,"
said the Horrobilly.
The mouse squeaked at him.
"All right, all right,"
said the Horrobilly.
"Don't lose your temper.
I'll try to change you
back into a person."

Just then Hairy Mary walked in.
"Aaaaaaaagh!"
screamed the Horrobilly,
and he fell off the cupboard.
"How dare you fall
off the cupboard!"
cried Hairy Mary angrily.

The Horrobilly was hanging
by his toes.
He had never been
the wrong way up before.
"At least you're not a mouse,
but something's gone wrong,"
he said.
"You've come back upside down."

All the children
laughed at the Horrobilly.
Hairy Mary lifted him down.
"You are silly,"
she said crossly.
"Go outside the classroom
until dinner time."

The Horrobilly was hungry.
First he ate up his own dinner.
Then he borrowed an apple,
and then a piece of cake.

When it was dinner time
the children couldn't find
their dinners.

The Horrobilly tried to hide.
But he had eaten so much
that his trousers split
with a loud noise.
"Who's there?" called a boy.
"Only us sandwiches,"
answered the Horrobilly.

"Come out, we know it's you,"
said the children.
They were hungry because
he had eaten their dinners.

"If we had some fish
we could have fish and chips –
if we had some chips,"
said the Horrobilly.
"I was just going to say
the same thing myself,"
said Hairy Mary.

She sent some children
to buy fish and potatoes.
"You were the greedy one
who ate all the dinners,"
said Hairy Mary
to the Horrobilly.
"So **you** must peel the potatoes."

"I'm sorry I can't let you
peel these potatoes,"
the Horrobilly said to
the children.
"It's such fun.
But Hairy Mary won't let
just **anybody** do them."

"We're not just anybody,"
said the children.
"We don't see why
you should have all the fun.
You must let us peel some."
"If you insist,"
said the Horrobilly.

"You **have** peeled
the potatoes quickly,"
said Hairy Mary.
"Think nothing of it,"
the Horrobilly boasted.
"They took me no time at all."

The fish and chips
were very tasty.
But the children laughed
because the Horrobilly
ate **another** dinner.

The next morning Hairy Mary
could not find the Horrobilly.
"I don't think I'll
go to school today,"
said a voice.
"Anyone who hides under the bed
must be a little potty,"
said Hairy Mary.

"They all laughed at me
because I ate so many dinners,"
said the voice sadly.
Just then there was a knock
at the door.
It was some children
on their way to school.
"Is the Horrobilly coming?"
they asked. "He's so nice,
he makes us laugh."

"They like me!"
shouted the Horrobilly.
"Did you hear that?
I'm going to school
and I'm taking my mice.
Don't try to stop me.
Wait for me, friends,
I'm coming!"